Make Your Own Art

Origami

Sally Henry and Trevor Cook

FRANKLIN WATTS

Published in 2011 by Franklin Watts

Copyright © 2011 Arcturus Publishing Limited

Franklin Watts
338 Euston Road
London NW1 3BH

Franklin Watts Australia
Level 17/207 Kent Street
Sydney, NSW 2000

Text and design: Sally Henry and Trevor Cook
Editor: Joe Harris
Photography: Sally Henry and Trevor Cook

Produced by Arcturus Publishing Limited,
26/27 Bickels Yard, 151–153 Bermondsey Street,
London SE1 3HA

British Library Cataloguing in Publication Data

Henry, Sally.
  Origami. -- (Make your own art)
  1. Origami--Juvenile literature.
  I. Title II. Series
  736.9'82-dc22

ISBN-13: 978 1 4451 0530 7

SL001624EN

Printed in China

Franklin Watts is a division of Hachette Children's Books,
an Hachette Livre UK company.
www.hachettelivre.co.uk

Contents

Introduction	4
Garden Bird	8
Lotus Flower	10
Jumping Frog	12
School of Fish	14
Duck	16
Windmill	18
Dinosaur	20
Tiger Lily	22
Pinwheel	24
Butterfly	26
Flapping Crane	28
Water Bomb	30
Glossary	31
Index and Websites	32

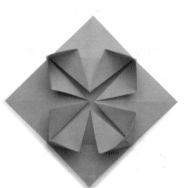

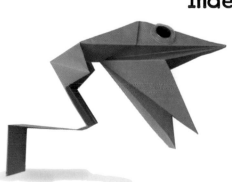

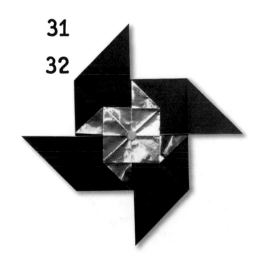

Introduction

The folk art of origami has been popular in Japan for hundreds of years. Now it is an art form loved around the world.

The idea is to make a work of art by folding just one sheet of paper. All you need is a clean, clear work space, clean hands and some paper!

Japanese origami paper squares

Paper

Origami paper needs to be strong so it can be folded and refolded many times without tearing. It shouldn't be too thick, as that would make folding many layers hard. Origami paper is usually square and colored on one side. It generally measures between 150–200 mm (6 and 8 inches) square.

Folds

Nearly all projects in origami have just a few kinds of folds. Learn the names of these and it will make the instructions easier to follow later on. We use symbols to explain what happens between the pictures. Learn what they mean as we go along.

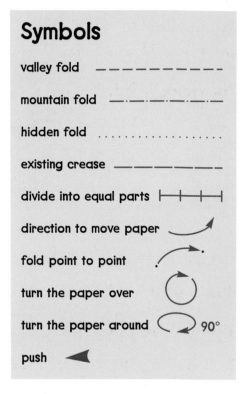

Symbols

valley fold	– – – – – – –
mountain fold	— · — · — · —
hidden fold	· · · · · · · · · · · ·
existing crease	—— —— ——
divide into equal parts	⊢——⊣——⊣
direction to move paper	↘
fold point to point	⤴
turn the paper over	↻
turn the paper around	↺ 90°
push	◀

Valley, mountain and book folds

1

2

The mark left by folding is called a crease.

3

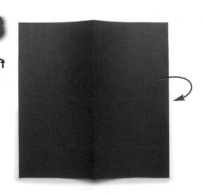

Here's a piece of origami paper. Fold it down the middle like this. We call this a **valley fold**.

Folding a square of paper in this way is called a **book fold**, because it makes a book shape.

If you fold the paper away from you instead, you get a **mountain fold**.

Cupboard fold

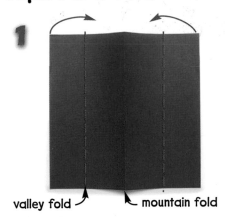

1 valley fold · mountain fold

Make a mountain fold down the middle of the paper and two valley folds as shown.

2

Fold the sides to the middle, using the centre crease as a guide. This is a **cupboard fold**.

3 equally spaced creases

Open the sides right out and you can see that we've divided the square into four equal parts.

Diagonal fold

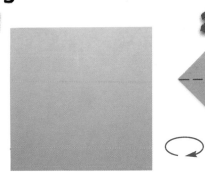

1

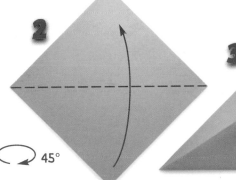

2 45°

3

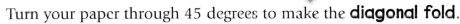

4

5

Turn your paper through 45 degrees to make the **diagonal fold**.

Inside reverse fold

1 Start with a diagonal-folded corner. Make a new valley fold across the end to make a crease.

2 Open the corner and change the new valley fold on the upper side into a mountain fold, and the mountain fold into a valley.

3 Gently ease the folded tip back inside as you close the main fold.

4 Finish by pressing down firmly.

1

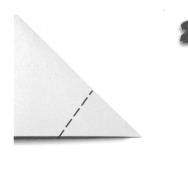

2

3 push in

2

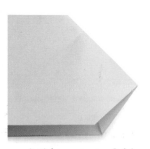

4 inside reverse fold

Outside reverse fold

1 Beginning with another diagonal-folded corner, mountain fold the end to make a crease.

2 Open the corner and convert the new mountain fold on the upper side to a valley fold and the existing mountain fold to a valley fold.

3 Ease the folded tip back over the corner, at the same time closing the main fold.

4 Press down to establish the new fold.

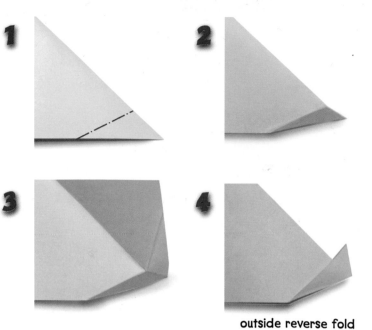

outside reverse fold

Bases

Many origami designs share the same early stages. They are often named after the most common designs to which they lead. Here are some common ones that will appear later in this book.

Kite base

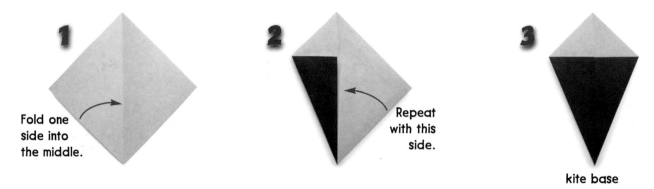

1 Fold one side into the middle.

2 Repeat with this side.

3 kite base

Start with a diagonal crease (see page 5, diagonal fold, picture 3).

Square base

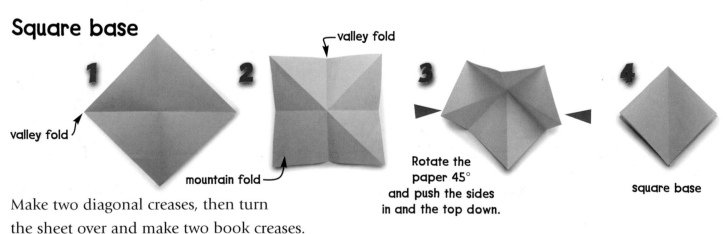

1 valley fold

2 valley fold — mountain fold

3 Rotate the paper 45° and push the sides in and the top down.

4 square base

Make two diagonal creases, then turn the sheet over and make two book creases.

Water bomb base

The same method that makes the square base can be used to produce the water bomb base. Fold the square like the square base, but reverse the folds.

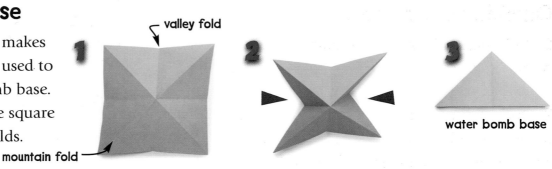

valley fold

mountain fold

water bomb base

Bird base

The bird base is named after the many bird designs that begin with it. Start with a square base.

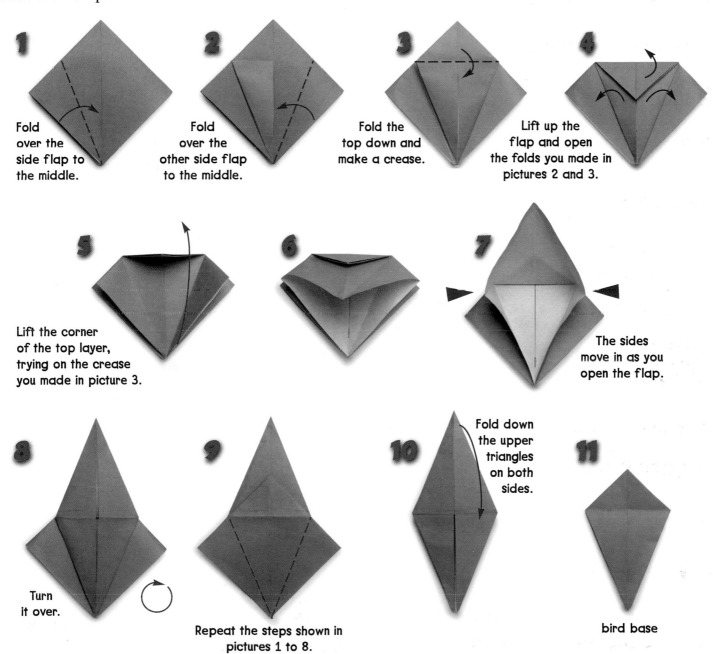

1 Fold over the side flap to the middle.

2 Fold over the other side flap to the middle.

3 Fold the top down and make a crease.

4 Lift up the flap and open the folds you made in pictures 2 and 3.

5 Lift the corner of the top layer, trying on the crease you made in picture 3.

6

7 The sides move in as you open the flap.

8 Turn it over.

9 Repeat the steps shown in pictures 1 to 8.

10 Fold down the upper triangles on both sides.

11 bird base

Garden Bird

Brighten up your garden with this colourful bird!

10 MINUTES

Start with a kite base (see page 6).

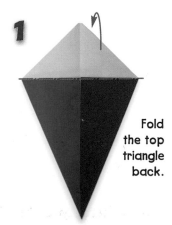
1

Fold the top triangle back.

2 Fold the top corners in to the centre and crease. Open the right one out again.

3 Fold the point shown out and down to create a valley fold.

4 Ease the flap out carefully.

5 Now do the same to the other side.

6 Make two folds.

7 Valley fold on the centre line.

8 Make creases on these lines.

45°

Turn the piece.

9 Valley fold this edge to make an inside reverse fold, see page 5.

mountain fold

valley fold

10 Combine the folds to make an inside reverse fold and an outside reverse fold.

11 Stand it up and add an eye.

12

And there's your bird!

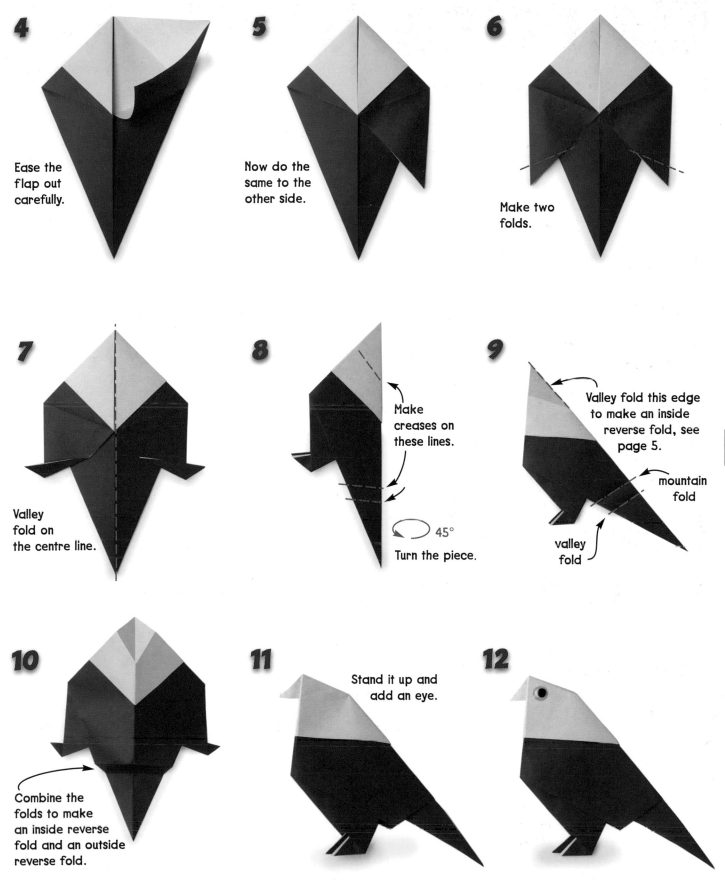

Lotus Flower

This flower makes a pretty table decoration!

10

Let's start with two diagonal folds (see square base, page 6, picture 2).

1

Fold the corners to the middle.

2

Turn the paper over.

3

Cupboard fold the top and bottom (see page 5).

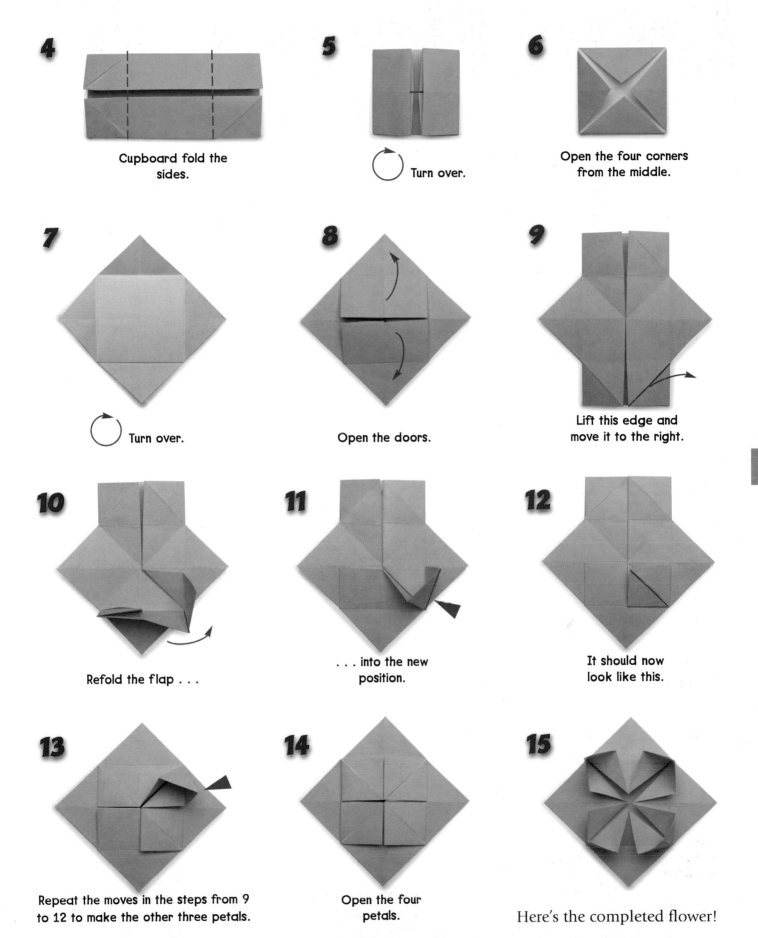

4 Cupboard fold the sides.

5 Turn over.

6 Open the four corners from the middle.

7 Turn over.

8 Open the doors.

9 Lift this edge and move it to the right.

10 Refold the flap . . .

11 . . . into the new position.

12 It should now look like this.

13 Repeat the moves in the steps from 9 to 12 to make the other three petals.

14 Open the four petals.

15 Here's the completed flower!

Jumping Frog

20 MINUTES

Fold a pair of frogs and have a jumping contest!

We're going to make two frogs from one paper square.

1 Cut the square exactly in two, then fold one of the pieces in half.

2

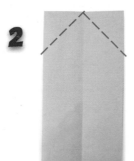

Fold the top corners to the middle.

3

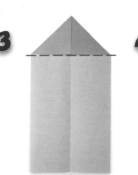

Open the folds, then fold the top down.

4

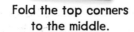

Fold the corners to the middle again.

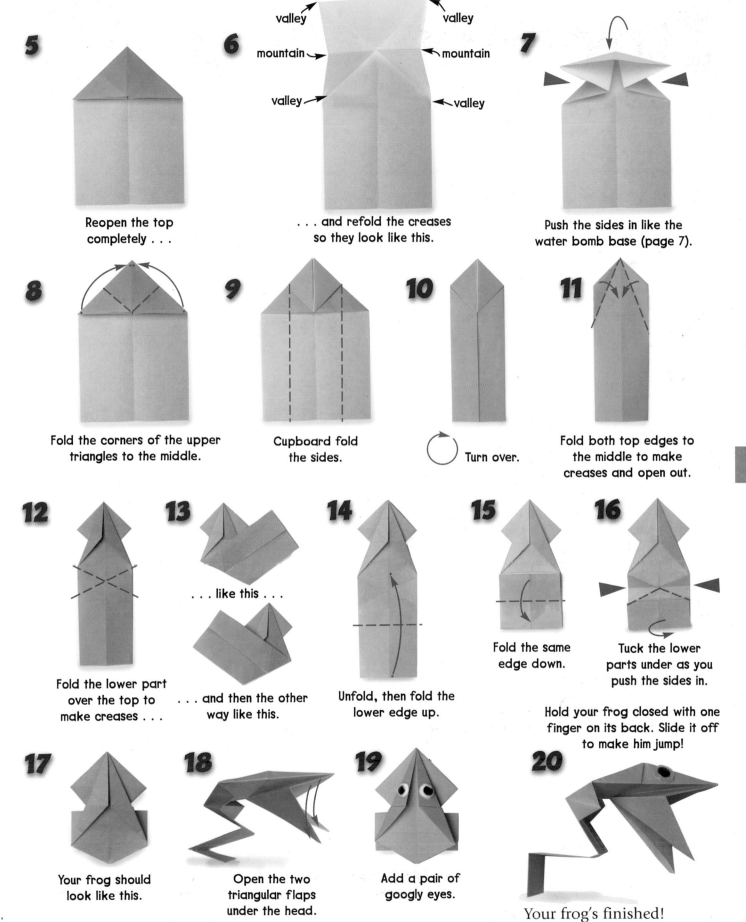

5 Reopen the top completely . . .

6 valley valley
mountain → ← mountain
valley → ← valley
. . . and refold the creases so they look like this.

7 Push the sides in like the water bomb base (page 7).

8 Fold the corners of the upper triangles to the middle.

9 Cupboard fold the sides.

10 Turn over.

11 Fold both top edges to the middle to make creases and open out.

12 Fold the lower part over the top to make creases . . .

13 . . . like this . . .
. . . and then the other way like this.

14 Unfold, then fold the lower edge up.

15 Fold the same edge down.

16 Tuck the lower parts under as you push the sides in.

Hold your frog closed with one finger on its back. Slide it off to make him jump!

17 Your frog should look like this.

18 Open the two triangular flaps under the head.

19 Add a pair of googly eyes.

20 Your frog's finished!

School of Fish

You can make a school of these colourful fish in no time!

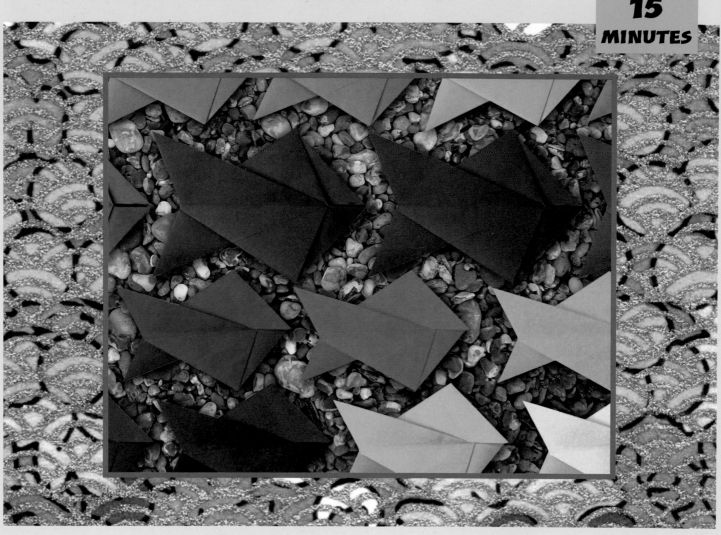

Start with an opened-up water bomb base (see page 7).

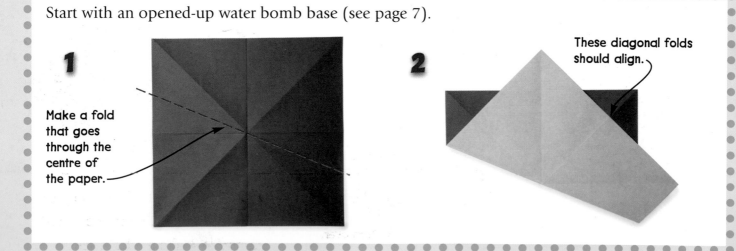

1

Make a fold that goes through the centre of the paper.

2

These diagonal folds should align.

3

Now follow the steps as though you were
making a water bomb base (see page 7).

4

You should end up with
a shape like this.

5

Holding the lower part down,
move the upper triangle around
to the left, using the new folds.

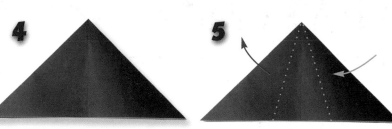

6

Turn the model.
70°

7

Fold along
this line.

8

Fold this
flap up.

9

Fold this
flap up.

10

Fold
the upper
triangular
flap down.

11

Turn over.

12

Here's your finished fish! Repeat
the steps with different-coloured
papers to make a whole school!

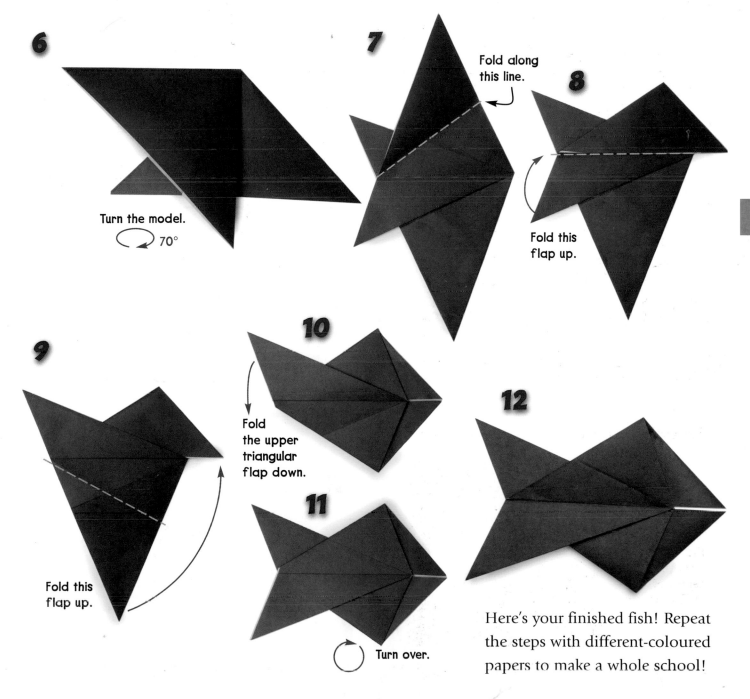

Duck

This looks just like a duck, but don't get it wet!

This duck is easier than it looks. The head's the key. Good luck!

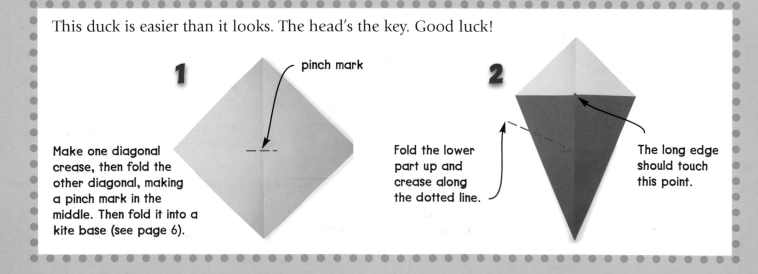

1

pinch mark

Make one diagonal crease, then fold the other diagonal, making a pinch mark in the middle. Then fold it into a kite base (see page 6).

2

Fold the lower part up and crease along the dotted line.

The long edge should touch this point.

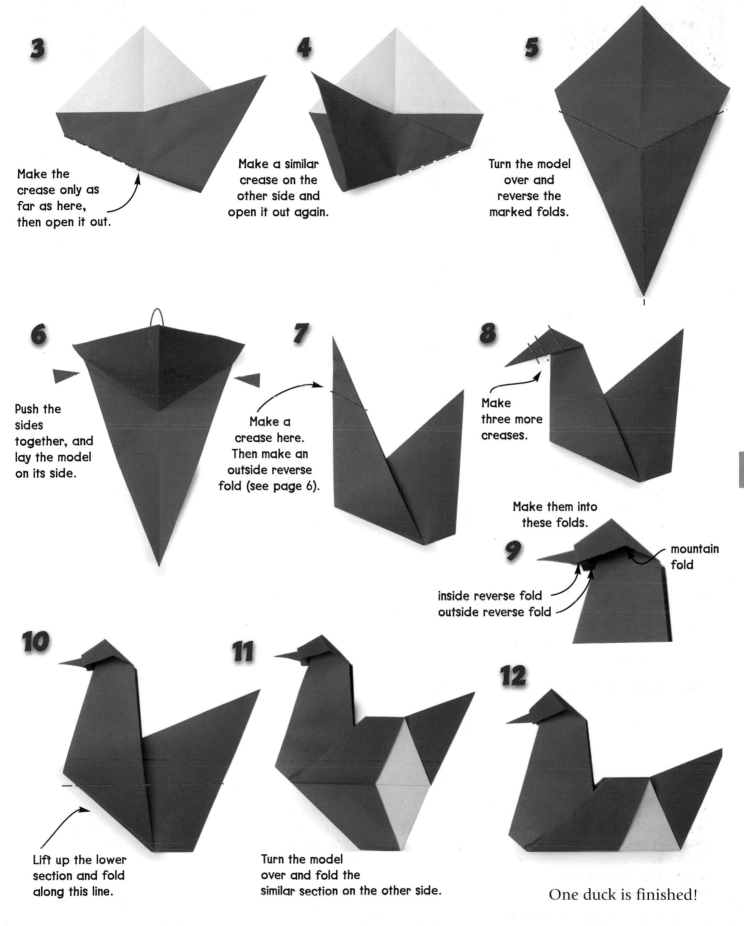

3 Make the crease only as far as here, then open it out.

4 Make a similar crease on the other side and open it out again.

5 Turn the model over and reverse the marked folds.

6 Push the sides together, and lay the model on its side.

7 Make a crease here. Then make an outside reverse fold (see page 6).

8 Make three more creases.

Make them into these folds.

9 inside reverse fold
outside reverse fold
mountain fold

10 Lift up the lower section and fold along this line.

11 Turn the model over and fold the similar section on the other side.

12 One duck is finished!

Windmill

You can make this windmill spin just by blowing on it!

This windmill starts with a cupboard fold (see page 5).

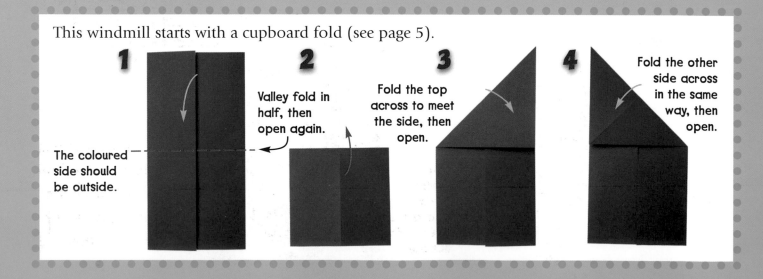

1 The coloured side should be outside.

2 Valley fold in half, then open again.

3 Fold the top across to meet the side, then open.

4 Fold the other side across in the same way, then open.

5

Fold the top down to meet the centre crease you made first.

6

Fold the bottom to the middle, then open the last two folds.

7

Fold diagonally across the middle, like this.

8

Open the last fold, then fold in the opposite direction, like this.

9

Open the top part in the direction of the arrows.

10

Open it out and down.

11

Flatten the top like this, then fold the lower part in the same way.

12

Fold up this triangle.

13

Fold up the triangle on the opposite side.

14

You should have this shape.

15

Make another windmill from a square with sides half the size of this one.

Ask an adult to help you fix your windmill to a stick with a drawing pin, and it's finished!

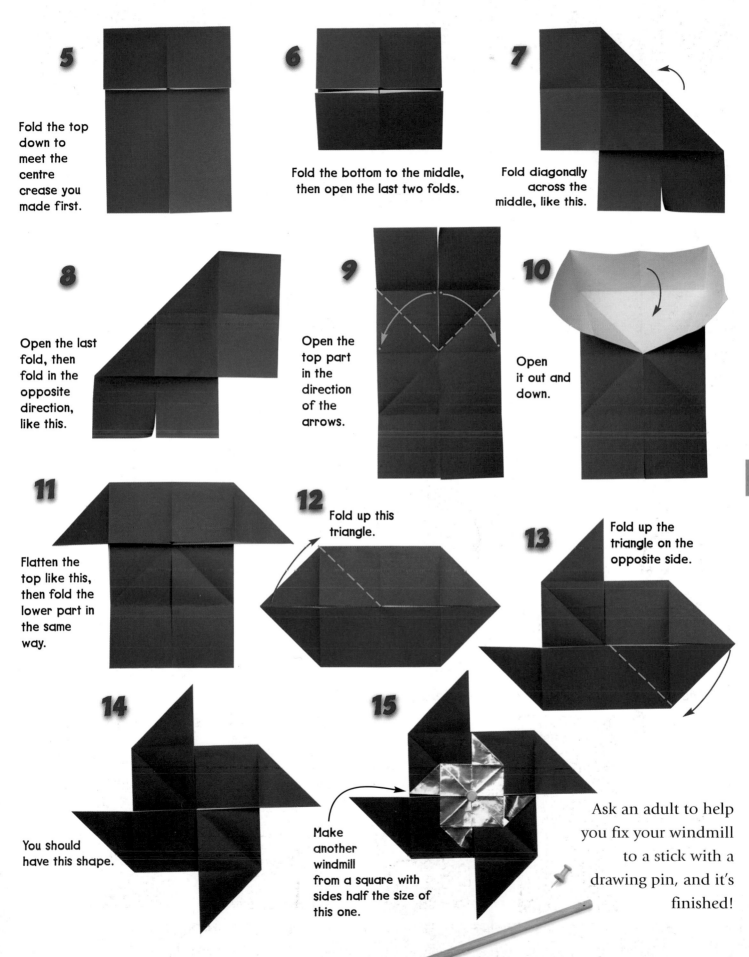

Dinosaur

From the age of the dinosaurs comes the huge seismosaurus!

20 MINUTES

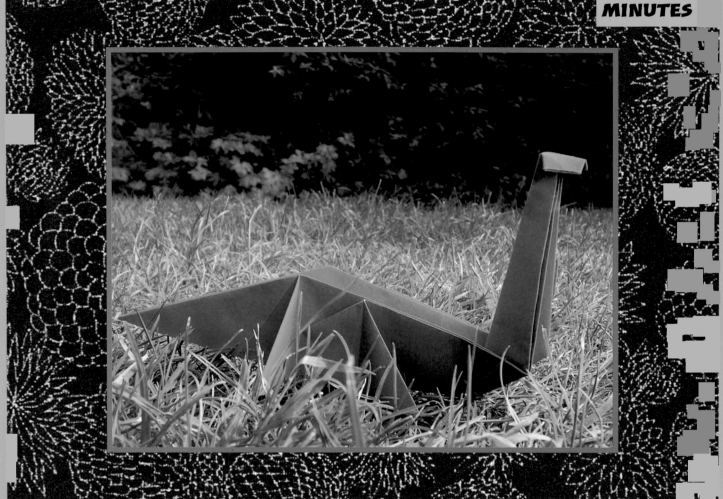

Start with a kite base (see page 6).

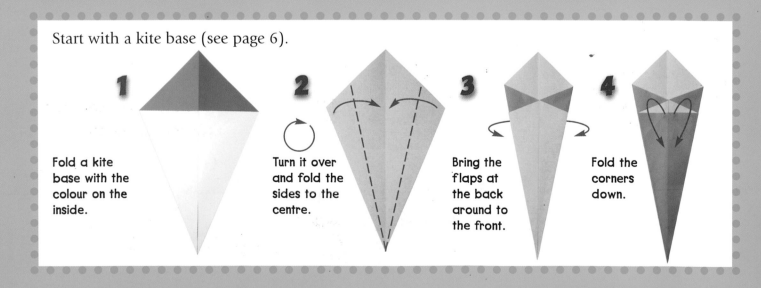

1 Fold a kite base with the colour on the inside.

2 Turn it over and fold the sides to the centre.

3 Bring the flaps at the back around to the front.

4 Fold the corners down.

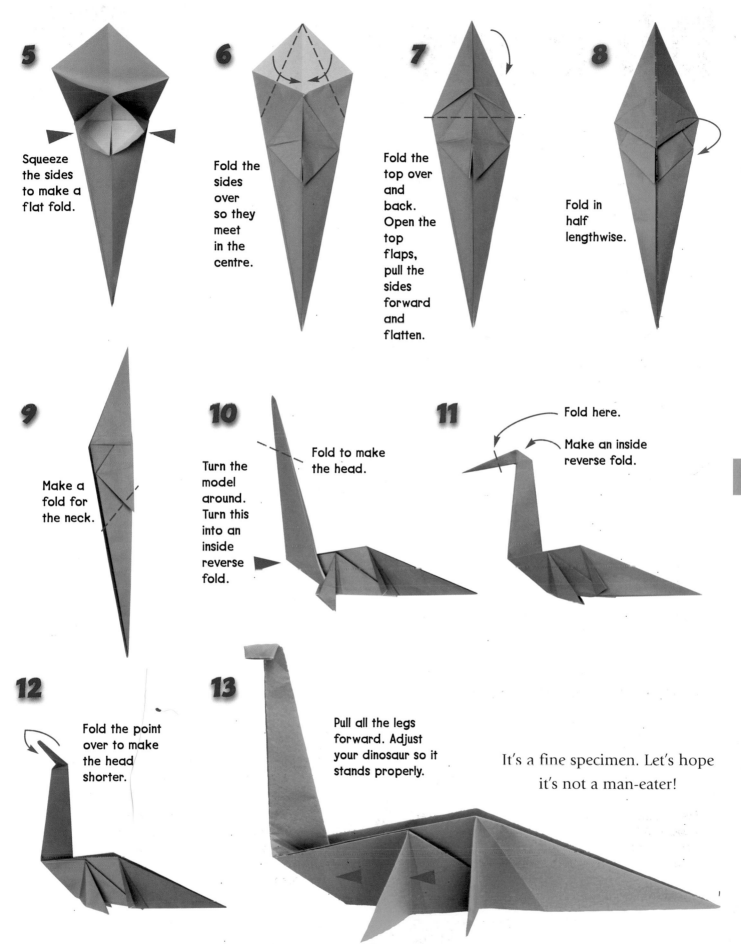

5 Squeeze the sides to make a flat fold.

6 Fold the sides over so they meet in the centre.

7 Fold the top over and back. Open the top flaps, pull the sides forward and flatten.

8 Fold in half lengthwise.

9 Make a fold for the neck.

10 Turn the model around. Turn this into an inside reverse fold.

Fold to make the head.

11 Fold here.

Make an inside reverse fold.

12 Fold the point over to make the head shorter.

13 Pull all the legs forward. Adjust your dinosaur so it stands properly.

It's a fine specimen. Let's hope it's not a man-eater!

Tiger Lily

You can enjoy these paper flowers all year.

20 MINUTES

Start with a square base (see page 6).

1

Lift up the upper flap on the left to turn on the centre line.

2

Open the flap and squash it down so the edge becomes the centre.

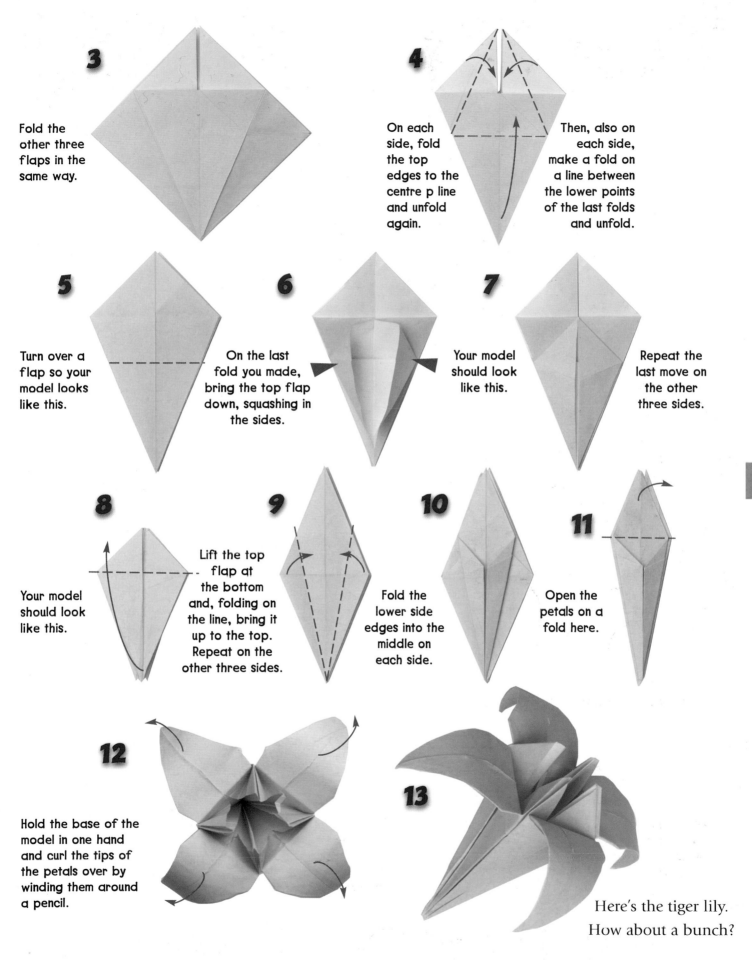

3 Fold the other three flaps in the same way.

4 On each side, fold the top edges to the centre p line and unfold again. Then, also on each side, make a fold on a line between the lower points of the last folds and unfold.

5 Turn over a flap so your model looks like this.

6 On the last fold you made, bring the top flap down, squashing in the sides.

7 Your model should look like this. Repeat the last move on the other three sides.

8 Your model should look like this.

9 Lift the top flap at the bottom and, folding on the line, bring it up to the top. Repeat on the other three sides.

10 Fold the lower side edges into the middle on each side.

11 Open the petals on a fold here.

12 Hold the base of the model in one hand and curl the tips of the petals over by winding them around a pencil.

13 Here's the tiger lily. How about a bunch?

Pinwheel

This wheel looks like a puzzle, but it's not as hard as it seems!

There are eight parts in this model, all folded in the same way.

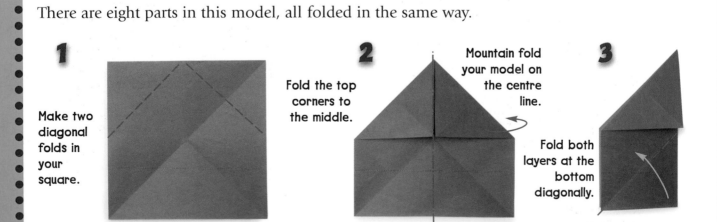

1 Make two diagonal folds in your square.

2 Fold the top corners to the middle.

Mountain fold your model on the centre line.

3 Fold both layers at the bottom diagonally.

4

Open out the model like this.

5

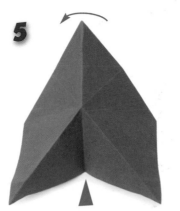

Reverse the fold at the bottom, push it in, and lay it flat.

6

The result should look like this.

Here's another.

7

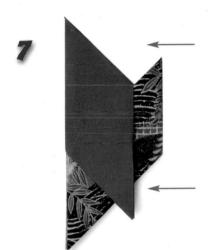

The second piece goes in the first piece like this.

8

Wrap the tip of the first piece around the second piece and tuck it in. Repeat on both sides.

9

Continue with more pieces.

10

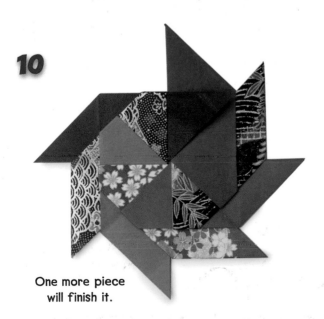

One more piece will finish it.

11

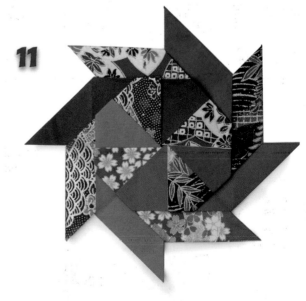

One pinwheel is finished!

Butterfly

Bring the garden indoors with this clever piece of folding.

26

Fold a water bomb base with the colour on the outside (see page 7).

1

Fold the top down to touch the bottom edge.

2

Make a valley fold here.

Make mountain folds here.

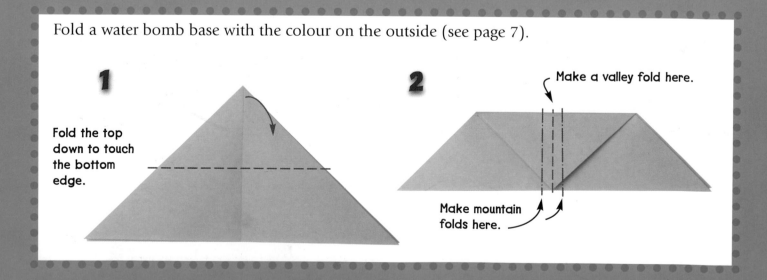

3

Now, unfold the model.

4

Fold two flaps
along these lines.

5

Fold two points under.

6

Open the two flaps and
the two points.

7

↻ 180°
Turn the model around.

Fold down the upper triangles on both sides.

8

Fold back the wing tips.

9

Make a
mountain fold
and a valley
fold at the tip of
each wing.

10

You've made a butterfly. Now make some more!

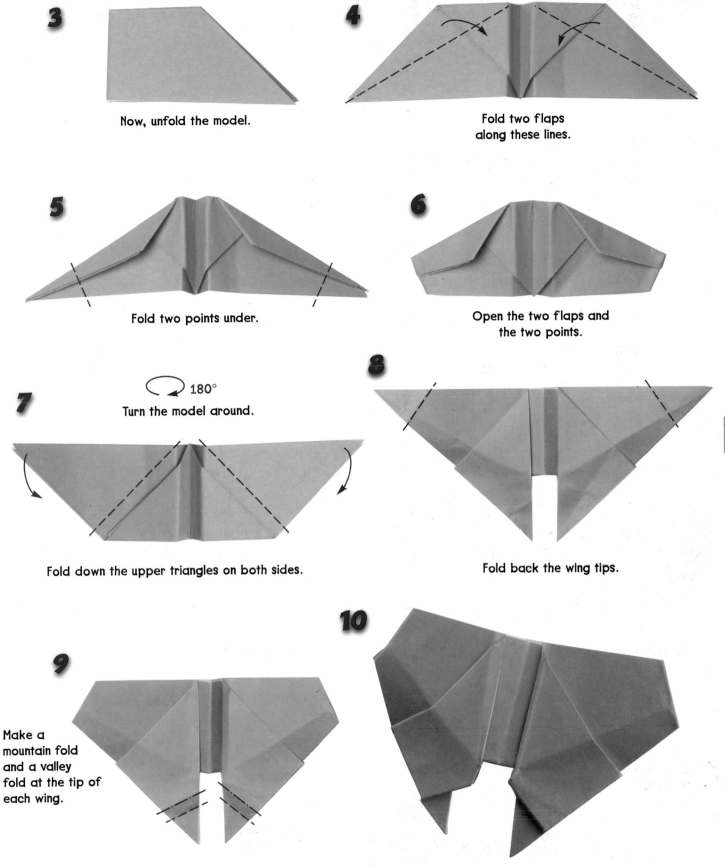

Flapping Crane

In Japan, origami cranes are believed to bring people good luck.

15 MINUTES

Start with a square base (see page 6). The open end should point down.

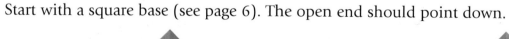

1

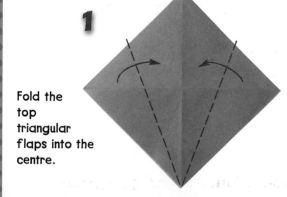

Fold the top triangular flaps into the centre.

2

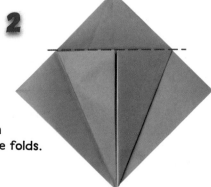

Make a fold with the top triangle, then open all three folds.

3

Open the point at the bottom of the square.

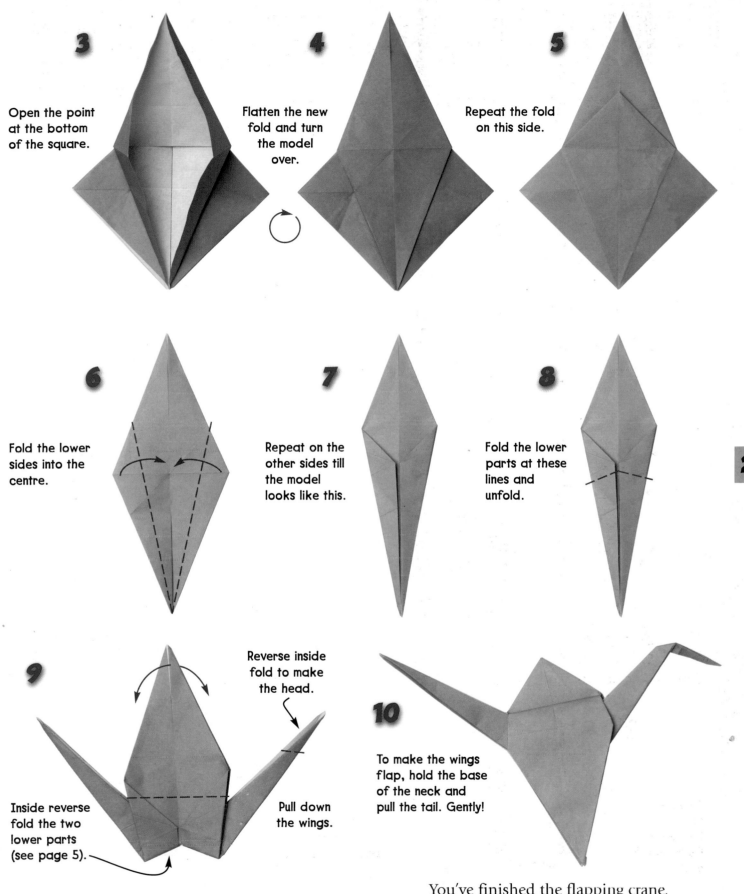

4

Flatten the new fold and turn the model over.

5

Repeat the fold on this side.

6

Fold the lower sides into the centre.

7

Repeat on the other sides till the model looks like this.

8

Fold the lower parts at these lines and unfold.

9

Inside reverse fold the two lower parts (see page 5).

Reverse inside fold to make the head.

Pull down the wings.

10

To make the wings flap, hold the base of the neck and pull the tail. Gently!

You've finished the flapping crane. It's a classic origami model!

Water Bomb

It's fun to make, but use it outside unless you want to have to clean up!

1

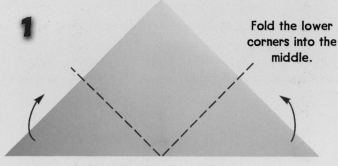

Fold the lower corners into the middle.

Start with the water bomb base, of course!

2

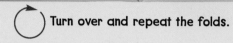

Turn over and repeat the folds.

3

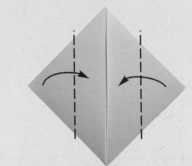

Fold the top layer points at the side into the middle.

4

Turn over and repeat the folds.

5

Fold the point on the top layer down.

6

Turn over and repeat the folds.

7

Put the point of this triangular flap into the pocket of the flap next to it.

Repeat for the other pocket, then repeat for both pockets on the other side.

8

Blow into the hole at this end to inflate the model. Fill it with water!

9

Here is the water bomb. The rest is up to you!

Glossary

base   A combination of folds that can be used as a starting point for creating an origami model.

bird base   A classic base formed by petal folding both sides of a square base.

contest   A game in which two or more people try to win.

crease   A line formed by folding paper.

designs   Decorative patterns.

divided   Broken apart or separated.

fold   To bring two parts of a sheet of paper together, usually flattening the paper.

googly eyes   Plastic stick-on eyes with moving parts, used for making toys.

instructions   Explanations or directions.

mountain fold   A crease formed by folding paper out, up and away from you.

origami   A Japanese word meaning 'folding paper'.

petal fold   A fold in which a layer is lifted up and the sides are narrowed to form a point.

reverse fold   A fold in which part of a flap is folded inside or outside another flap.

rotate   To move in a circle.

square base   A simple base that uses just four creases.

squash   A method in which a flap is separated and flattened.

symbols   Objects or pictures that stand for something else.

valley fold   A crease made by folding paper in, down and towards you.

waterbomb base   A simple base that uses the square base creases.

Index

bases 6, 7, 8, 10, 14, 15, 16,
  20, 22, 26, 28, 30

bird bases 7

book folds 5, 6

butterflies 26–27

creases 4, 5, 6, 7, 8, 9, 13,
  16, 17, 19

cupboard folds 5, 18

diagonal folds 5, 10, 14, 24

dinosaurs 20–21

fish 14–15

flapping cranes 28–29

folds 4, 5, 6, 7, 8, 9, 10, 12,
  14, 15, 17, 19, 21, 23

frogs 12–13

garden birds 8–9

inside reverse folds 5, 9,
  17, 21

jumping contests 12

kite bases 6, 8, 20

lotus flowers 10–11

mountain folds 4, 5, 6, 9,
  17, 26, 27

outside reverse folds 6, 9,
  17

paper 4, 9, 17, 21

pinwheels 24–25

reverse folds 5, 6

schools 14, 15

seismosaurus 20–21

square bases 6, 22, 28

table decorations 10

tiger lilies 22–23

valley folds 4, 6, 7, 9, 26

water bombs 7, 30

wings 29

Websites

http://easyorigamiforkids.com
  Follow these videos to make amazing origami items.
www.origami-kids.com/paperairplanes-1-tumbling.php
  Make a squadron of paper aeroplanes to fly.
www.enchantedlearning.com/crafts/origami
  Fold paper to make hats and whales on this site.